THE McKINDLESS GROUP

DAVID DEVOY

*To Alistair
Best Wishes
David Devoy*

First published 2019

Amberley Publishing
The Hill, Stroud
Gloucestershire, GL5 4EP

www.amberley-books.com

Copyright © David Devoy, 2019

The right of David Devoy to be identified as the Author of this work has been asserted in accordance with the Copyrights, Designs and Patents Act 1988.

ISBN 978 1 4456 9115 2 (print)
ISBN 978 1 4456 9116 9 (ebook)

All rights reserved. No part of this book may be reprinted or reproduced or utilised in any form or by any electronic, mechanical or other means, now known or hereafter invented, including photocopying and recording, or in any information storage or retrieval system, without the permission in writing from the Publishers.

British Library Cataloguing in Publication Data.
A catalogue record for this book is available from the British Library.

Origination by Amberley Publishing.
Printed in the UK.

Introduction

The McKindless bus company was founded in Newmains by Vincent and Margaret (known as Pearl) McKindless after selling their haulage business around ten years earlier. It started off as a small operation of a few buses, a lorry and two coaches in 1987, and traded under the name of Chartered Coaches. Its aim was to provide school contracts and private hires, but it quickly moved into local bus operation, spurred on by the problems suffered by its larger neighbour, Central Scottish. The management tried to change the work, pay and conditions of their staff, but were met by a strike. No sooner had that been settled than the workforce again withdrew their labour. This vacuum led to the appearance of many small operators, and McKindless were no exception. Their first service operated in 1989 during the industrial unrest. Seeing potential, they registered service 60, linking West Crindledyke and Wishaw/Hamilton on a half-hour frequency on Mondays to Saturdays. At first no fares could legally be charged for the first forty-two days of the emergency service, but a bucket for donations was used.

A second route began from 11 January 1990, when service 67, linking Motherwell and Bonkle, was launched. A couple of former Highland Scottish Fords and some early ex-Ribble Leyland Nationals formed the early bus fleet. Service 67 was extended from 11 April and ran to Hamilton bus station. As all the early buses had a red livery, this was adopted as standard. Glasgow city centre was reached from 19 November, when some journeys on service 64 from West Crindledyke were extended to terminate in Cadogan Street. The first double-decker was an ex-Grampian Daimler Fleetline, which was soon joined by an ex-Southern Vectis Bristol VRT. Further Leyland Nationals were also added from Stagecoach.

January 1991 saw the Traffic Commissioners cancel all of the company's service registrations. Services continued to run on a free basis, with public donations. By the middle of the month, a new licence was issued to Margaret McKindless, and all services were reintroduced from 8 February. Meanwhile, the early Fords had been replaced by more Nationals. The network changed in July, with service 66 being extended from Hamilton to Shotts; meanwhile, Glasgow service 64 was cancelled and two new routes were added. Service 61 ran from West Crindledyke to Newarthill, and service 68 linked West Crindledyke and Pather. More Nationals were acquired from Stagecoach for use on the Shotts service and had their stripes repainted in two shades of green. A tendered service numbered 335 was taken over and ran between Cardowan and Gartcosh, replacing Strathclyde Buses.

By September 1992, the operational fleet consisted of seven Nationals, one Bristol VRT, one Ford coach and one Leyland Atlantean. Service 68 was revised to operate from West Crindledyke to Hamilton via Craigneuk from 29 March 1993. An ex-Eastern Scottish MCW Metroliner joined the fleet and received McKindless Express logos. At this point, negotiations were ongoing regarding the sale of the services and the company was trying to diversify into coach hire.

In March 1994 the commercial routes and six buses were bought by Kelvin Central Buses. KCB were the successors to Central Scottish and had been building their market share by purchasing competing businesses in the area. A clause in the contract stated that the company could not register any commercial bus services for a period of two years. The cash paid for the services was ploughed into the business, allowing the land that the Bogside depot stood on to be purchased outright. Two oddball Bedfords were purchased for school contracts.

To all intents and purposes, the company fell off the radar and quietly got on with their contracts. Towards the end of 1995, another couple of Nationals appeared. From August 1996 they started a commuter shuttle between Newmains and Glasgow, offering up to eight return journeys a day and running under the McKindless Express brand, using vehicles in a blue and grey livery that was based on the old British Airways colour scheme. Graham Park joined the company as Transport Manager; he had previously worked for Cumberland Motor Services.

On 24 April 1997, the company returned to commercial service work with service 9, linking Hamilton and Cleland, service 10, linking Waterloo and Bonkle, and service 68, linking Hamilton and West Crindledyke, all of which operated on a half-hourly frequency. In addition, the express service was altered to run from West Crindledyke and Glasgow Buchanan bus station. From February 1998, Volvo-engined Leyland Nationals began to be stockpiled while they awaited upgrading with new seats and back and front end modifications. In March some received the blue and grey express livery and even had televisions installed. The heavier weight at the rear later caused some back ends to crack.

The fleet now stood at fifty-two vehicles. More services were added, including the 12 from Wishaw to Parkside, the 44 from Bellshill to Newarthill and the 93 from Parkside to Forgewood. Many of the Leyland Nationals were coming to the end of their lives and started to be withdrawn from the end of 1999 onwards. Lightweight Dennis Darts were appearing, and offered much better fuel consumption. Service 56 was added to the portfolio and linked Glasgow to Shotts, reactivating another old Central SMT route number. More coaches were acquired to upgrade the Glasgow Shuttle service, which ran in competition with Hutchison's of Overtown. The legal address for the fleet was The McKindless Group, McKindless Business Park, 101 Main Street, Newmains, North Lanarkshire.

A series of one-day strikes by Stagecoach Western staff resulted in the company's vehicles operating on hire to Strathclyde PTE in March 2000, covering school contracts and service 354, which linked Girvan and Barr in Ayrshire. A new service 41 was introduced from 15 May, linking Carluke and Hamilton, and replaced a Firstbus route in the area. The Leyland Lynx was introduced to the fleet at this time, but never achieved the popularity of the earlier Leyland Nationals. Eight former Blackpool Optare City Pacers were also added to the fleet, and fleet numbers started to appear on the vehicles around July. A special vehicle added was AEC Routemaster ALD 966B, which was painted into Central SMT colours with adverts for the various McKindless businesses, and was a birthday present to Vince from his wife Margaret. The company licence at this time was for sixty vehicles, but around seventy-two were actually owned. Another operator licence was issued to a newly started company – McKindless Bus Company Ltd of Main Street, Newmains – in November 2000, and this allowed for the operation of twenty more vehicles. The reason for this would soon become apparent.

2001 began with the registration of another new service, when route 67 began running from Hamilton to Glasgow from 15 January. A batch of ex-London MCW Metrobuses were being converted to single-door, using a plain metal panel with no glazing, allowing a two-seat bench seat to be added. Further Dennis Darts continued to enter service, replacing Leyland Nationals and offering superior fuel consumption figures. Another new type acquired was the Optare MetroRider, with a small batch being purchased from Go-Ahead Northern. The larger Optare Delta also made an appearance in the fleet at this time. The fleet numbering system fell into disuse around May. Quite a lot of redundant buses were removed by Dunsmore of Larkhall which freed up space for the ever-expanding fleet. Moreover, a second depot was opened in Seath Road, Rutherglen, after school contracts were obtained in the Glasgow area. MCW Metrobuses began to appear on service 67 on a regular basis. A former Bus Group Alexander-bodied Leyland Leopard that had been converted for use as a tow-wagon was obtained from a preservationist; numbered 1949, it was put to work in Central SMT-style livery.

2002 saw the company conquer new territory when route 80 was registered, which would begin from 22 January. This new service ran from Glasgow to Kirkintilloch on a fifteen-minute frequency, and ran in competition with First Glasgow. Second-hand buses continued to be added to stock on a regular basis. A Wright-bodied Volvo B7TL demonstrator appeared for a few days in August, and was used on the 41 service from Hamilton to Lanark. A small batch of ex-East Yorkshire Optare Excels also became available and joined the fleet around September, and these were the company's first low-floor buses. Additionally, a former Southern Vectis Bristol Lodekka was added to the heritage fleet. A contract was obtained from SPT to run a shuttle after the Glasgow Subway drivers went on strike for a week in November. Six Metrobuses were provided to run links from Govan Cross, Partick and Shields Road to the city centre.

In 2003, a travel shop was opened at Parkhead Cross in Glasgow's East End, which seemed a little strange as no services actually passed it; however, this may have been a clue as to further, future intentions. More low-floor buses were sourced from Menzies Aviation and began to be stockpiled and refurbished at Newmains depot. A new service was registered to begin on 24 April, wholly within Glasgow, and this would also operate on a fifteen-minute frequency. It was numbered 75 and competed with First Glasgow for its entire route. It followed the southern section of First Glasgow service 45 and coupled this with the northern section of their route 75, linking Kennishead and Milton via the city centre. A new source for second-hand low-floor buses produced several Marshall-bodied Dennis Darts that had originated on the Isle of Man. These were followed by more from London. Planning permission was granted for a new bus depot at Parkhead in Glasgow in early 2004. Some temporary contracts were obtained when HAD Coaches of Shotts collapsed on 5 March, and some vehicles were also taken into stock for school contracts. 13 April saw service 44, from Bellshill to Wishaw, being extended to Overtown, ramping up competition with Hutchison's Coaches. Service 22 was also started between Coltness and Overtown from 13 April. SPT tendered service 317, running from Hamilton to Lanark, was registered to run as service 31 on a commercial basis from 25 April. From 28 September, services 60/A were renumbered as X1, Glasgow to West Crindledyke, and X2, Glasgow to Cleland, respectively. The fleet now stood at around 120 vehicles. The entire fleet of Berkhof-bodied Dennis Lances were advertised by dealers around November, and the first pair to leave the fleet passed to Wilson's of Gourock. Three step-entrance Darts made the trip in the reverse direction.

2005 started off with some step-entrance Darts arriving from Stagecoach Wales and Metrobus of Orpington, and the Routemaster was sold for continued preservation. New premises were under construction at Nuneaton Street in Parkhead and were intended to replace Rutherglen depot. On 21 April a new service was launched between Glasgow Cross and Faifley. Service 62 would compete with First Glasgow over the entire route and against other independents over various other sections. The 62 route quickly became their best route and was operated by low floor vehicles when enough had arrived. Counteracting this were some changes to the Lanarkshire operations. Service 44, operating between Bellshill and Overtown, was cut back to serve Coltness and Wishaw on a half-hour frequency, while service 68 had its Hamilton end of the route changed to serve North Motherwell instead. Services 41 and 56 also had their frequencies reduced from every ten to every fifteen minutes. Six double-deckers were hired again to SPT for subway replacement duties on various dates. A few more MCW Metrobuses were purchased for school contracts between May and August and would all receive the yellow livery. August also saw a BMC Falcon being demonstrated to the company on the Lanark service. The year closed with the acquisition of an Alexander ALX-bodied Volvo B6LE from Burnley & Pendle, and further examples would appear in due course.

   2006 brought more low-floor Plaxton Pointer Darts from London. Service 24, the Wishaw to Coltness circular, was renumbered as service 4; the reason for this was that the highly respected Hutchison's of Overtown had used this number in the Coltness area before it was withdrawn. The Scottish Government extended the provision of its concessionary fares scheme, allowing over a million people over sixty, and also those with a disability, to access free travel at any time of the day. However, the scheme to reimburse operators would be capped. A second-hand Optare Excel entered service in all-over white with advertising for Cascia Property, which was a new business venture set up by the McKindless family in March 2006. This company had previously been known as Brakemotto Limited from 23 December 1998 until 5 February 1999, and was registered at 89 North Orchard Street, Motherwell, ML1 3JL. It was dissolved in July 2015. Just before a change in ownership, thirteen buses were acquired from First Stop Travel of Renfrew in May, although some were only used as a source of spares. Unusually, among the buses were some Marshall midibuses, of which two entered service. The under-performing service 24 was finally withdrawn on 17 July, with service 68, running from West Crindledyke to Hamilton, following on 22 July. On a brighter note, new service X21, linking Lanark and East Kilbride, started on 21 August, and service 31, running from Lanark to Hamilton, had its frequency doubled. Meanwhile, more Optare Deltas were being taken into stock. The first ever vehicle purchased new arrived in September, when a Chinese-built King Long took to the road, closely followed by a pair of BMC Falcons. All three were supplied by Auto Holdings (dealer). Coaches working on the East Kilbride X21 service had their lettering changed to read Express Shuttle.

   February 2007 saw the addition of some Leyland Olympian double-deckers from Stagecoach Glasgow, while March witnessed some Volvo B6s arrive from UK North. Meanwhile, service 62 was extended from Glasgow Cross to Parkhead Forge from 4 April. The competition changed locally when Hutchison's Coaches announced the sale of their stage carriage services to Firstbus in June. The recent extension of service 62 was withdrawn once again from 9 July. Many more buses were being added from both Stagecoach and ComfortDelGro Aerdart fleets. Resources were redirected when service X21 was withdrawn in September, and new service 6 was registered. This linked Motherwell to North Motherwell and ran over a route previously operated by Hutchison's. Interestingly, some Optare Excels were purchased from Hutchison's to operate it, and these retained the blue livery with McKindless fleet names added. The King Long was returned to BMC, Coventry (dealer), in October, being replaced by another BMC Falcon. More double-deckers intended for school contracts were added around the same time. Route 41 was upgraded when some new ADL Enviros entered service in December.

   March 2008 saw newly introduced service 6 withdrawn after competition with First Glasgow proved to be ill-advised. Some Mini-Pointer Dennis Darts were acquired in June, and many redundant buses were removed for scrap. November brought a couple of Optare Excels from Nottingham.

   Further contraction of activities in February 2009 saw the cancellation of services 67 and 80. These ran from Glasgow to Little Earnock and Harestanes respectively. Rumours began to surface that all was not well with the company, but they were denied at the time. A new style of fleet name appeared in March. The express services to Glasgow were also reduced quite considerably, with service X2 being withdrawn completely and X1 reduced to a weekday peak-hour operation only. There was a strange occurrence when Leyland Olympian G536 VBB was taken from the scrap line and repainted into a smart livery of white and purple, separated by a lime green band. There was some speculation at the time, but it remained a mystery for a while. The remaining journeys on service X1 were withdrawn in November and with that the blue and grey coach livery disappeared. Metrobus B299 WUL was repainted into a version of the livery used on the single-deckers and received the new style fleet names. Meanwhile, the mysterious Olympian and two other double-deckers passed to a new company, which traded as JMB Travel and operated from the same premises at Newmains.

The company ceased operation of its services abruptly at 1900 hours on Friday 19 February 2010. Many employees were not notified that the company was about to close, only discovering this when their shifts ended, and with the end of the company 116 people were left unemployed. There were also allegations of tax fraud, with the Inland Revenue telling former employees that the company had not paid tax or national insurance contributions on their behalf since 2004.

A spokesperson for McKindless said: 'It was with great regret that McKindless Express and McKindless Bus Company Ltd were forced to cease trading on Friday, February 19, 2010. Due to the current economic climate, rising fuel costs, and falling revenue due to local authority reductions in school contracts and on our local service routes due to the continued blatant predatory action of a dominant operator, we were no longer in a position to continue trading.'

Latterly, six commercial routes were in operation, requiring around forty-five vehicles. Police were waiting with management as there were fears of trouble when the drivers returned to the depot after their last shift. They received one week's wages along with their P45s. At this time, the company was still awaiting the result of a Public Inquiry held three months earlier by the Traffic Commissioner.

Strathclyde Partnership for Transport officials placed posters on over 500 bus stops to inform the public about replacement services, which were provided by other operators.

It later transpired that the McKindless Bus Company Limited was a company incorporated in the British Virgin Islands on 1 January 2001, having its registered office at Geneva Place, Waterfront Drive, PO Box 3469, Road Town, Tortola BVI, British Virgin Islands and having its principal place of business at 39 Nuneaton Street, Glasgow G40 4JT.

McKindless Bus Co. No. 2 Limited was incorporated on 10 August 2004, with the registered office being located in Geneva Place. This company went on to trade for thirteen years and ten months.

So ended a major presence in the Scottish independent bus scene. While the company is now gone, it is not forgotten.

Thanks to my daughters Samantha and Jennifer for their help with the technical stuff, and for proof reading. Thanks also to the McKindless family for all their help over the years.

KHG 193T was a Leyland Atlantean AN68/1R/East Lancs H45/33F purchased new as Hyndburn Transport number 193 in September 1978. On disposal it passed to Wright's of Wrexham, then passed through the hands of Rowe & Tudhope of Kilmarnock and Irvine's of Law before joining the McKindless fleet. It was only used as a school bus, and was seen parked between runs at Bogside depot.

NTC 626M was a Leyland National 1151/1R B49F purchased new by National Bus Company subsidiary Ribble Motor Services as their number 446 in January 1974. It was manufactured in large quantities between 1972 and 1985, and was developed as a joint project between two UK nationalised industries – the National Bus Company and British Leyland. Buses were constructed at a specially built factory at the Lillyhall Industrial Estate, Workington. Styling was carried out by the famed Italian vehicle stylist Giovanni Michelotti.

HDL 411N was a Bristol VRT/ECW H39/31F new as Southern Vectis 649 in May 1975. It joined McKindless in 1990, and was captured in Motherwell while working on service 66 to Newmains. Originally intended to be designated the Bristol N-type, the chassis became known as the Bristol VR, an abbreviation for 'Vertical Rear', a reference to the layout of the transverse engine. A drop-centre rear axle and low frame were employed to keep the height of the vehicle down.

VKE 566S was a Leyland National 11351A/1R B49F new as Maidstone & District number 3566 in September 1977. It became Hastings & District number 566, Chesterfield Transport number 206, East Midland number 206 and North Western number 465 before reaching the McKindless fleet. It had been re-engined with a Volvo engine and refurbished both inside and out by the time of this picture, however. It would pass to Lothian Buses as their number 137 before passing into preservation.

NDZ 3138 was a Dennis Dart 8.5SDL/Wright Handybus B29F new as London Buses DW138 in February 1993. It became part of Stagecoach East London for a spell before transferring to Stagecoach Red & White as their number 468. It was re-registered as K983 CBO in February 2003 and was renumbered as Stagecoach West & Wales 32238 before its sale to 2-Travel, Swansea, in October 2004. It was then resold to the McKindless Group and is shown in Glasgow.

F177 LVU Mercedes Benz 609D/Made to Measure C22F was purchased from ex-Wiffen of Finchingfield in June 1994. It was on a private hire to Dumfries when snapped at Brooms Road car park. The coach livery was based on the colour scheme of British Airways.

JDZ 2411 was a Dennis Dart 9SDL/Wright B36F new as London Buses DWL11 in December 1990. It passed to Westlink in January 1994 and later worked for London United. It was acquired by McKindless in March 2000 and received fleet number D111, as shown in this view taken in Motherwell. The London DWL class managed to seat thirty-six by inserting a standard window bay instead of a short one.

H105 THE was a Dennis Dart 8.5SDL/Plaxton Pointer B28F new as London Buses DR5 in May 1991. London Buses ordered 153 units on the shortest chassis, which featured a split doorway, giving a low step for the less agile, but a higher front step, allowing a decent front clearance. With a 7-foot 6-inch width, they were a go-anywhere bus. This one was bought by McKindless in April 2000 and received the fleet number D117.

BYW 435V was a Leyland National 10351A/2R B36D new as London Transport LS435 in 1979. On disposal in December 1993 it was bought by Stuart Palmer, Dunstable, and was resold immediately to The Eden of West Auckland to be their N5, being re-registered as RJI 5755, with the centre doors removed. In 1996 the company was taken over by United, and the bus was allocated fleet number 3503. United in turn became part of Arriva North East, and the bus was put on the disposal list. In March 1998 it passed to Dart Buses of Paisley, who had access to the list as they were 23 per cent owned by Arriva Scotland West. It was immediately resold to McKindless and fitted with a Volvo engine – even being badged as a Volvo B10M! It carried the fleet number VN211 briefly.

KJD 527P was a Leyland National 10351A/2R B36D new as London Transport LS27 in August 1976. It was converted to single-door DP42F arrangement in 1986 for use on service X99 in London. It passed to Stuart Palmer, Dunstable, in July 1993 and The Eden (County Durham) three months later, where it was re-registered as RJI 5344. It was bought by Dart Buses of Paisley in January 1998 from Arriva North East and passed to McKindless two months later. It is seen in the coach version of the livery.

K351 SCN was an Optare MetroRider MR03 B26F new as Gateshead & District number 351 in March 1993. It was working on service 67 and had arrived at its terminus in Glasgow when this photograph was taken. The MCW Metrorider, launched at the 1986 Motor Show, was a minibus designed and built by Metro-Cammell Weymann (MCW) between 1986 and 1989. MCW's designs were offered for sale in 1989 and the rights to the MetroRider were bought by Optare. The Optare MetroRider was subsequently relaunched and continued in production until 2000.

Ex-Isle of Man Dennis Dart R681 OYS was receiving attention by the roadside in Oswald Street in Glasgow city centre when seen. In attendance were Volvo tow wagon E698 SWW and the Parkhead depot service van. The bus had been working on service 75, and was about halfway along the route when a fault occurred.

P157 BUG was an Optare Excel L1000 B36F new as Stanwell Buses XL7 in June 1997. It was bought by McKindless from London United in June 2003 and was re-registered WIL 9228. It had a very short life, however, and was cannibalised in August 2008. The Excel was launched in 1995 as one of the first low-floor single-deck vehicles, and approximately 600 were built. Power came from a Cummins 6BT, a six-cylinder turbo diesel engine, and the power was transmitted via an Allison B300R gearbox.

H161 NON was a Dennis Dart 8.5SDL/Carlyle B28F new as London Buses DT161 in February 1991. In November 1994 it became part of the privatised London United fleet, then joined McKindless in 1999. It later received fleet number D106 and was re-registered as RIL 9664. It was sold to First Stop Travel of Renfrew in July 2003 for further service.

OST 259S was a Ford R1114/Alexander Y Type B53F purchased new by Highland Omnibuses as their T159 in November 1977. On disposal it joined the fledgling McKindless of Wishaw operation and was captured here in Hamilton as it headed back to West Crindledyke on service 64. The Ford R-series was a range of chassis that evolved from designs made by Thames Trader in the mid-1960s. A number of components were shared with the D-series lorry, including the engine, which was mounted vertically at the front of the vehicle.

L168 YAT was a Dennis Dart 9SDL/Plaxton Pointer B34F new as London Buses DRL168 in February 1994. It passed to the privatised London United in October 1994, then Westlink in August 1999. It was acquired by McKindless in August 2004 and served the company for six years. With the launch of the Dennis Dart in 1989, Plaxton's subsidiary Reeve Burgess made the Pointer body on the short 8.5-metre chassis. The modular nature of both chassis and body resulted in various permutations, with 8.5-metre, 9.0-metre and 9.8-metre variants being manufactured.

EJR 122W was a Leyland Atlantean AN68C/2R/Alexander AL Type DPH45/33F new as Tyne & Wear PTE number 122 in December 1980. On disposal it passed to Mitchell's of Plean, then to Davies of Plean in 2000 and Wilson's of Strathaven in 2002, before reaching McKindless. It simply had the blue areas of its livery repainted into fleet livery and was pressed into service on school contracts.

GGE 162T was a Leyland National 10351A/1R B41F new as Greater Glasgow PTE number LN7 in February 1979. It moved to Southend Transport as their number 719. It was acquired by McKindless in 1997 and was one of two buses given an advert for the associated baby shop business. The location was Wishaw town centre.

E36 EVW was a Leyland Lynx LX112 B49F new as Colchester Corporation number 36 in February 1988. It passed to British Bus with the business and was transferred to Crosville Wales as their number SLC36. It was purchased by McKindless in 2000, and was one of four Lynxes operated. It carried fleet number LX603, as shown in this view taken in Hamilton.

The Bristol VRT featured a choice of either a Gardner 6LX or 6LW engine, or the Leyland O.600 engine. The transmission was a semi-automatic unit by Self-Changing Gears. Again originally intended to be designated the Bristol N-type, it became known as the Bristol VRT, an abbreviation for 'Vertical Rear Transverse'. RAU 809R began life with Trent, while HDL 411N was new to Southern Vectis.

R102 VLX was a Marshall Minibus B26F new as Centrewest ML102 in July 1998. It was an integral version of the low-floor Capital, based on Marshall's own chassis, and was launched in 1996. It was ultimately considered to be a failure due to low sales, with just thirty-six being produced, coupled with poor reliability. R102 VLX came from First Stop Travel in 2006, and was passing through Motherwell when seen.

D123 HHW was a Volvo B10M-61/Duple 320 C53F purchased new by Turner's of Bristol in February 1987. It was acquired by McKindless in 1994 for use on the Glasgow Express services, and was re-registered as JIL 5144. Duple announced a new coach model, known as the 300-series, in 1985. Sadly, by 1988 Duple's output was just 250 bodies, and the following year the business closed down, ending seventy years of tradition.

BX55 NYG was a BMC Falcon 1100 B40F built as a demonstrator for BMC of Coventry in January 2006. BMC is one of the largest commercial vehicle manufacturers in Turkey, and its products include buses, trucks and military vehicles. The company was founded in 1964 in partnership with the UK's British Motor Corporation. It was taken over by Çukurova Holdings of Turkey in 1989, and seized by the Turkish Government's TMSF in 2013.

J614 KCU was a Dennis Dart 9.8SDL/Wright Handybus B40F new as Tynemouth & District number 8014 in January 1992. It passed to McKindless in 2001 and was captured turning into Glassford Street in Glasgow while working on service 67. The body, which was built between 1990 and 1995, featured a bolted aluminium structure with two alternative windscreen styles. Go-Ahead Northern bought over eighty, and many later served in Scotland.

AMS 513K was a Leyland Leopard PSU3/3R/Alexander Y Type C49F new as Alexander (Midland) MPE 113 in May 1972. It passed to Kelvin Scottish and then Kelvin Central Buses as a tow-wagon, before being purchased by the McKindless Group. It received the dark red and cream livery and looked like an old Central SMT vehicle.

OAH 552M was a Leyland National 1151/1R B52F new as Eastern Counties LN552 in October 1973, and passed to Cambus when the company was split. By 1987 it was with Tyrerbus of Nelson; it moved to Franks of Haswell, then to Yorkshire Terrier as their number 20 in June 1989. It became Chesterfield Transport number 102 and was re-engined using a Volvo unit. It became North Western number 461 in 1997, and joined the McKindless Group the following year. It later became Lothian Buses number 134 in 2002 and passed to Rapson's Coaches in 2003 as their number 180.

HRP 672N was a Bristol VRT/ECW H74F new to United Counties as their 832 in April 1975. It passed to Stagecoach with the business, before later passing to Stagecoach Perth as their 102. On disposal in 1993 it passed to Marshall's of Baillieston for school contracts. It later passed to Stuart's of Carluke, then McKindless of Wishaw in 1998.

N421 PWV was a Plaxton Pointer-bodied Dennis Dart that started life as GU 5924 with Citybus in Hong Kong. It was imported to the UK by Stagecoach and became Hampshire Bus number 41, with the UK registration N421 PWV. McKindless acquired it in 2007, and it was seen at Partick in Glasgow while working on service 62.

A batch of eight Optare City Pacers were purchased from Blackpool Transport and were used very briefly. SIL 4784/5 are seen at the depot in Newmains. These were built on Volkswagen LT55 van chassis, which at the time were not available in the United Kingdom. The design was only moderately successful due to its high price, with around 300 being produced. The original registrations for this pair were F582 WCW and E567 GFR.

McKindless sold their commercial services along with several Leyland Nationals to Kelvin Central Buses in 1992. They remained in business, however, mainly on schools and contracts, but a little tendered work was also obtained. During this period PGE 817Y, a Bedford VAS/Marshall obtained from the MOD, joined the fleet, and it was seen at the company's Bogside depot.

PJJ 343S was a Leyland National 10351A/1R B41F purchased new by East Kent as their 1343 in September 1977. It passed to Delta of Kirkby in Ashfield as their 631, and was re-registered to VY 2150 before becoming AFG 317S and being disposed of to the McKindless Group. It was captured in Wishaw while working on service 9 in June 1997.

E116 UTX was a Leyland Lynx LX112L B51F new as Merthyr Tydfil Transport number 116 in July 1988. It joined McKindless in 2000 from Arriva Cymru. It had also worked in Yorkshire for West Riding Group subsidiaries Yorkshire Buses and South Yorkshire Road Transport. The fleet numbering scheme was short-lived, and this shot was taken in Motherwell town centre.

K104 SAG was a Dennis Dart 9SDL/Plaxton Pointer B28F new as London Buses DRL104 in April 1993. It passed to London United on privatisation in October 1994. It was purchased by McKindless in September 2002 and ran for around seven years before being scrapped. It was captured in Glasgow on service 80, bound for Harestanes.

SJ04 DZZ was a Transbus Dart SLF B29F purchased new by Stuart's of Carluke in August 2004. It passed to McKindless in 2009, and was turning into Hope Street in Glasgow when seen. The company ceased operation of its services at 1900 hours on Friday 19 February 2010. On disposal, SJ04 DZZ joined Humphreys Coaches/New Adventure Travel in Wales.

S556 OGB was an Optare Excel L1070 B39F purchased new by Hutchison's of Overtown in January 1999. McKindless and Hutchison ran in competition on various routes, but the owning Anderson family decided to retire and sold their business to First Glasgow in early 2007. McKindless purchased four of these buses from Hutchison's in October and simply changed the fleet names to compete with Firstbus.

GAO 708N was a Leyland National 11351/1R B52F that was new as Cumberland number 366 in November 1974. It was caught here at Craigends, on the outskirts of Glasgow. This bus passed to Kelvin Central Buses as their number 1172 when McKindless sold the stage services in 1994.

F551 SHX was a DAF SB220L/Optare Delta B30D new as London Buses DA2 in June 1989. It lost its centre doorway and gained extra seats after just a year in its original guise. It was re-registered as A5 LBR in March 1993 and transferred to London United two years later. On passing to McKindless in 2000 it was re-registered again as RIL 9868 and received the fleet number DA601.

V211 ENU was an Optare Excel L1150 B46F purchased new by Trent as their number 211 in February 2000. It was passing 'Dissie' corner in Glasgow, which was so named as it was a regular place for meeting your date. If they didn't like the look of you, they wouldn't show up, and this was known as a 'Dissie', or 'Disappointment'. V211 ENU, however, had no such problem.

A new source of second-hand vehicles was tapped when a batch of Plaxton Pointer B30D-bodied Dennis Dart SLFs were obtained from Aircoach, Dublin, in 2007. DLA7 still retained its former owner's livery as it awaits its turn in the paint shop. It would receive UK registration number Y392 LCS in due course.

D507 RCK was a Mercedes L608D/Reebur DP19F new as Ribble number 507 in October 1986. It passed to Dart Buses of Paisley, then moved to McKindless in 1997 for use on the express services to Glasgow. The management of Dart were on good terms with the company and even did the schedules for them.

This Volkswagen LT55/Optare City Pacer B19F was new to Blackpool Transport in 1987 as E567 GFR, and ran until withdrawal in 2000, when it was sold to McKindless. It is seen in Motherwell on the short local service to Cleland, but it was destined to have a short life in Lanarkshire, however, as the fleet standardised on Dennis Darts and MCW Metroriders.

A busy scene in central Glasgow shows Optare Excel YBZ 1462 overtaking Dennis Dart P723 RYL. They were working on services 62 and 75 respectively, which both ran in competition with First Glasgow services. The Egyptian Halls in the background is a Category 'A' listed building, built between 1870 and 1872 and designed by Alexander 'Greek' Thomson, a talented Scottish architect regarded as a pioneer in sustainable building.

SN51 UDW was a Dennis Dart SLF/Plaxton Pointer B29F purchased new by HAD Coaches of Shotts in November 2001. It passed to Irvine's of Law in 2004, and then to McKindless five years later. It would later pass to Midland Choice as number 2251, then Arriva Midlands as their number 2103.

London buses have traditionally been a popular second-hand buy for independents. McKindless were no exception and bought many MCW Metrobuses from the capital, allowing modern vehicles to be acquired at a reasonable price. Low-floor buses were quite expensive as not too many were available pre-owned. A batch of Berkhof-bodied Dennis Lances were obtained from Menzies Aviation services after being replaced on Heathrow Airport duties.

SJ04 DZY was a Transbus Dart SLF B29F purchased new by Stuart's of Carluke in August 2004. It passed to McKindless and was heading for Milton on service 75 when photographed. It was destined to have a short life after it was involved in a towing incident, which apparently damaged the rear end. A replacement engine was sourced but never fitted as the company were struggling to survive by this time and it was simply abandoned.

E919 EAY was a Volvo B10M-61/Plaxton Paramount C53F delivered new to Henry Crawford Coaches of Neilston in August 1987. It passed to Galloway's of Harthill before reaching McKindless in 2001. It received the express livery and was captured on the Glasgow Shuttle as it approached Buchanan bus station. Regulars on this service received a complimentary box of chocolates at Christmas.

L158 WAG was a Dennis Dart 9SDL/Plaxton Pointer B34F new as London Buses DRL158 in September 1993. It became part of the privatised South London fleet in 1994 and then passed to Arriva London. McKindless obtained a batch of these from Ensign (dealer) in March 2005 and there they remained until the demise of the company in 2010.

UEO 478T was a Leyland National 11351A/1R B49F new as Barrow Corporation number 16 in August 1978. It passed to Cumberland as their number 761 before reaching McKindless in 1992, with whom it was seen working as a school bus in Motherwell. It later returned to Barrow for preservation, but was used as a source of spares for other buses.

A700 UOE was an MCW Metrobus DR102/27 H43/30F new as West Midlands PTE number 2700 in November 1983. On disposal it passed to Thorpe's of Perivale. It joined the McKindless group in 2005 and was a dedicated school bus. It later passed to JMB Travel, Andrews of Leicester and Bill's Coach Hire of Milton Keynes.

C662 LFT was a Leyland Olympian ONLXB/1R/Alexander R Type H77F new to Tyne & Wear PTE as their number 662 in March 1986. It later moved to Stagecoach Transit and subsequently to Stagecoach Western in 2002. It ran in Glasgow in Magicbus livery for a while before returning to Ayrshire, and was acquired by McKindless in 2007. It was photographed passing through Motherwell while working service 9.

M181 UAN was a Dennis Lance SLF/Berkhof 2000 B37D purchased new by Speedlink Airport Services for use at Heathrow Airport in July 1995. It passed to Menzies Aviation Services when the contracts changed hands. It was acquired by McKindless in 2003, and re-registered as WIL 9206. It was working on service 75 when snapped in Jamaica Street in Glasgow.

YPJ 502Y was a Leyland Olympian ONTL11/2RSp/ECW CH45/28F purchased new by Alder Valley as their 1502 in May 1983. It passed to Northern Bus and Stephenson's of Rochford before joining McKindless in 1999. It was re-registered as HJI 3932 and received coach livery.

M420 PVN was a Volvo B6-50/Alexander Dash B40F purchased new by OK Travel in October 1994. It passed to the Go-Ahead Group with the business, and was sold to McKindless in 2007. It had just arrived in Glasgow on a 67 service when seen and would terminate in Killermont Street before heading back to Lanarkshire.

N322 JTL was a Volvo B6-50/East Lancs B44F new as Roadcar number 322 in October 1995, and passed to Stagecoach with the business. It was purchased by McKindless in 2007, and was passing through Shawlands Cross on a 75 service, bound for Kennishead, when seen. This section of the route paralleled a section of the First Glasgow 45 service.

M507 ALP was a MAN 11.190/Optare Vectra B42F that was new to R&I Tours, London, as their number 249 in May 1995. MTL London Northern took over R&I's buses in June 1996, but later passed them to Metroline of Harrow. This bus passed to McKindless in 2002 and was joined by a similar ex-demonstrator the following year.

M189 UAN was a Dennis Lance SLF/Berkhof 2000 B37D purchased new by Speedlink Airport Services for use at Heathrow Airport in July 1995. It passed to Menzies Aviation Services when the contracts changed hands. It was acquired by McKindless in 2003, and is shown before it was refurbished and repainted into fleet livery. It would later be re-registered as WIL 9203.

K889 BRW was a Volvo B10M-60/Plaxton Premiere C53F delivered to Bonas, t/a Supreme of Coventry, in January 1992. It passed to Alex Head Coaches of Lutton and ran as PIL 2863 and 7195 BY for a spell. It returned to its original number for disposal to McKindless in 2005. It ran in its as-acquired colours, but would be repainted in due course.

A543 HAC was a Leyland Olympian ONLXB/1R/ECW H45/32F new as Midland Red (South) number 903 in August 1983. It was one of seventeen of these purchased by this operator. It was transferred to Stagecoach Devon as fleet number 14943 before joining McKindless in 2007, and was snapped in Hamilton on a school contract.

J711 CWT was a Volvo B10M-60/Plaxton Premiere C48Ft purchased new by Wallace Arnold Tours of Leeds in April 1992. On disposal it passed to Titterington's of Blencow, before joining McKindless in 2001. It was re-registered as YIB 1189 in June 2001, but then changed the same month to YIB 4528 for some unknown reason. This shot shows it working on the Glasgow Shuttle.

G741 RTY was a DAF SB220L/Optare Delta B49F new as Northern General 4741 in August 1989. It was acquired by McKindless in 2006 from Go North East, joining many similar buses sourced from various operators. The Delta was launched in 1988 and ceased in 1999, with a grand total of 324 examples being built.

G512 VYE was a Dennis Dart 8.5SDL/Duple Dartline B28F new as London Buses number DT12 in April 1990. It passed to the privatised London United in November 1994 and was fitted with coach seats, luggage racks and air conditioning for Airbus Direct services in June 1995. It passed to McKindless in August 2004 and was crossing Jamaica Bridge in Glasgow when photographed.

The story of the Plaxton-bodied Dart is one of amazing success. The conservative body that Plaxton subsidiary Reeve-Burgess put on the Dennis chassis was an instant success. They began to sell like hot cakes, and production soon shifted to Plaxton's main works at Scarborough. This one was new to London Buses in May 1991, and was bought by McKindless in April 2000. It was scrapped in 2009.

R95 HUS was an Optare Excel L1070 B39F purchased new by Hutchison's of Overtown in April 1998. It would remain in the fleet until October 2007, when it passed to McKindless of Wishaw. As Hutchison's had sold their services to Firstbus, it was thought that some goodwill could be obtained by keeping Hutchison's colours, which were well-respected in the area.

NEO 830R was a Leyland National 11351A/1R B49F new as Barrow Corporation number 12 in April 1977. McKindless purchased it from Cumberland and merely adapted the Stagecoach livery, as shown in this view taken in Wishaw. The National was an integrally constructed British bus manufactured in large quantities between 1972 and 1985. It was developed as a joint project between two UK nationalised industries – the National Bus Company and British Leyland. Buses were constructed at a specially built factory at the Lillyhall Industrial Estate, Workington.

The McKindless Group

L254 CCK was a Volvo B6-50/Alexander Dash DP40F new in January 1994 as Ribble number 254. It was transferred to Stagecoach Cleveland before sale to UK North. UK North, an operator in the Manchester area, had their licence revoked over safety fears after several buses were involved in accidents. L254 CCK was resold to the McKindless Group, and was captured crossing Jamaica Bridge in Glasgow.

UHG 723R was a Leyland National 11351A/1R B49F new as Ribble 723 in September 1976. It later passed to Cumberland and was converted to B17DL to allow for the carrying of wheelchairs. It was acquired by McKindless in 1992 and entered service in its old colours as DP45F, as shown in this view taken in Wishaw while it was working on service 66, bound for Hamilton.

R691 OYS, a Dennis Dart SLF fitted with Marshall Capital bodywork, was new as DMN 21R with Isle of Man Transport. It was one of a batch purchased by McKindless and was re-registered in the UK before entering service in 2004. It is shown passing through Hamilton town centre while working on the 56 service.

P343 JND was a Volvo B6LE-53/Alexander ALX200 B36F new as Greater Manchester South number 343 in February 1997. It passed to Stagecoach Ribble and then to Burnley & Pendle as their number 208 when the Lancashire operations were sold by Stagecoach. It is shown in Hamilton bus station while working on the 31 service to Lanark.

J634 KCU was a Dennis Dart/Wright Handybus B40F purchased new by Go-Ahead Northern as their number 8034 in March 1992. It was acquired by McKindless in 2001, and was pictured in Glasgow with a defective electronic destination screen. London Buses was the largest customer of the Handybus, buying a fleet of nearly 200, while Go-Ahead Northern bought over eighty, and Ulsterbus and Citybus had forty between them.

B109 WUL was an MCW Metrobus DR101/17 H43/28D new as London Regional Transport M1109 in December 1984. Ten years later it passed to the privatised Leaside Buses, which was later rebranded as Arriva London. It was acquired by McKindless in November 2001, and stayed in the fleet for seven years. It then passed to Shoreline Suncruisers of Scarborough for use as an open-topper.

LG02 FFE was a Dennis Dart SLF/Plaxton Pointer B29F new as London United DPK621 in May 2002. It joined the McKindless Group in June 2008, and was caught in Dumbarton Road in Glasgow while working on the 62 service. In April 2010 it was bought by Your Bus of Nottingham. In October 2012 it then passed to the Rotala Group, Birmingham, for their Diamond Bus operations before its eventual sale to Britannia of Northampton in July 2016.

OPC 222W was a Volvo B10M-61/Van Hool Alizee C50F purchased new by Syway of Cranleigh in April 1981. It joined McKindless in April 1998 as MRL 493P from Ambassador of Yeaden, and was working on the express service to Coltness when seen. Ironically, the registration plate made the vehicle appear to be older than it actually was.

P340 JND was a Volvo B6LE-53/Alexander ALX200 B36F new as Stagecoach Manchester number 340 in February 1997. It passed to Ribble and was sold to Blazefield on 15 April 2001, when four garages and 230 buses changed hands. It passed to McKindless in 2005, and is seen with the final version of the fleet name as it turns into Argyle Street in Glasgow.

L167 YAT was a Dennis Dart 9SDL/Plaxton Pointer B34F new as London Buses DRL167 in February 1994. It joined McKindless in September 1994 and was captured in Trongate in Glasgow while working on the 62 service. The screen has already been changed for the return journey to Faifley. Dennis originally codenamed the Dart project as DM88 and it was duly launched as the Dart midibus at the 1988 NEC Commercial Vehicle motor show.

Y286 LCS began life as 01-D-34168 with Aircoach of Dublin. It was purchased by McKindless in 2007 and given its UK registration number. It retained its two doors and internal luggage racks, and this left room for just thirty seats. It later passed to WJC Coaches before being resold to Howards Travel Group, where it was given a major refurbishment.

NEL 861M was a Leyland National 1151/1R B49F purchased new by Hants & Dorset as their 3618 in November 1973. It became part of the Hampshire Bus fleet and passed into Stagecoach ownership with the business. It was transferred to Cumberland before sale to Vincent McKindless in 1990, and was caught in Hamilton bus station while working on service 66 to Bonkle.

K621 PGO was a 9-metre Dennis Dart/Plaxton Pointer B35F new to Metrobus of Crawley in 1992 and was acquired via Ensign (dealer) in 2004. It was pictured in Trongate in Glasgow city centre. Ensignbus have been in business for forty years and during those years have sold over 20,000 buses to nearly 100 countries, have undertaken around 25,000 MOT tests, have converted over 1,000 buses to open top and have carried out over 5,000 single-door conversions.

J952 MFT was a Dennis Dart 9.8SDL/Wright Handybus B40F new as Northern General number 8052 in August 1992. On disposal it passed to Dennis's of Dukinfield, then was acquired by First Stop Travel of Renfrew before reaching McKindless in 2006. It was captured in Union Street in Glasgow while working on the 75 service.

GPC 732N was a Leyland National 11351/1R 01740 B49F new as Alder Valley number 183 in November 1974. It passed with Newbury depot to Newbury Buses, which was part of Reading Buses. On disposal it joined Classic Buses of Annfield Plain, and passed with the services to Go-Ahead Northern. It was acquired by McKindless in 1998 and was snapped in Hamilton.

V195 DRC was an Optare Excel L1150 B43F new as Trent 195 in September 1999. It passed to McKindless in 2006 and was caught in Partick. Optare can trace its origins to 1923, when Charles H. Roe started bus-body building at Cross Gates in Leeds. The company was purchased by Leyland in 1962. Optare was formed by a buyout from Leyland Truck & Bus in 1985, and by 2018 Ashok Leyland owned 99.08 per cent of the shares.

H102 THE was a Dennis Dart/Plaxton Pointer B28F purchased new by London Buses Ltd in April 1991 as their DR2. It passed to London United in 1994 before reaching McKindless in 2000 and was seen in Hamilton. The amount of information displayed in the front of the bus would be frowned upon nowadays as it impairs the driver's vision.

N324 JTL was a Volvo B6-50/East Lancs 2000 B44F new as Roadcar number 324 in October 1995. Roadcar was a member of the Yorkshire Traction Group until it was taken over by Stagecoach in December 2005. The smaller groups often used less popular coachbuilders as they could gain greater influence on their own specifications. This bus joined McKindless in 2007.

M958 SDP was a Dennis Lance SLF/Berkhof B33D purchased new by Speedlink Airport Services in April 1995. Berkhof is a Netherlands-based bus and coach builder, founded in 1970 by Arthur Berkhof and his son Henk. They started with only ten employees in a 1,000 square metre factory. During the first eighteen months the company only carried out bus repairs. In 1985, the operation moved to Valkenswaard, and in 1997 the company changed its name from Berkhof Groep to Berkhof Jonckheere Groep. In 1998 the whole company was bought by the VDL Groep.

L242 CCK was a Volvo B6-50/Alexander Dash DP40F new as Ribble number 242 in December 1993. It was acquired by UK North of Manchester. In early 2005 it revived the GM Buses name, and operated on routes 42, 86 and 192. It had its licence revoked and this bus passed to McKindless in 2006. It was resting in Lanark bus station at the southern terminus of route 41 when seen.

The McKindless Group

DDW 431V was a Leyland National 10351A/1R B41F new as Cynon Valley number 31 in January 1980. In 1992 Western Travel purchased Cynon Valley, which operated services in the Aberdare and Merthyr Tydfil areas, along with forty-six buses. DDW 431V passed to Classic of Annfield Plain and later Northern General, but joined McKindless from Hall of Kennoway in 1997, and was passing through Motherwell town centre when captured.

NDZ 3133 was a Dennis Dart 8.5SDL/Wright Handybus B29F new as London Buses DW133 in February 1993. It was transferred to Selkent in May 1998, then moved to Stagecoach Red & White as their number 463. It was re-registered to K21 CDW in 2003, and passed to McKindless the following year. It was turning into Howard Street in Glasgow, while working on the 62 service, when seen.

R281 EKH was an Optare Excel L1150 B45F new as East Yorkshire 281 in August 1997. It was still only six years old when McKindless purchased it, but was soon re-registered as YBZ 7531, as shown in this view taken in Chalmers Street in Clydebank. Optare is a Latin word, meaning 'to choose'.

A980 SYF was an MCW Metrobus DR101/17/MCW H43/28D new as London Transport M980 in February 1984. It became part of the privatised London United fleet in November 1994. It was numbered DD458 by McKindless on acquisition in November 2000, and was converted to single-door, as shown in this view taken in Motherwell. It was sold for scrap in 2009.

G990 KJX was a DAF SB3000/Van Hool Alizee C51Ft purchased new by Elsey of Gosberton in May 1990. McKindless purchased it from Hogg of Bearsden and it was resting at Bogside depot when photographed. It would receive the registration plate SIL 1816 in 2002. Van Hool was founded in 1947 by Bernard van Hool in Koningshooikt, near Lier, Belgium.

H880 LOX was a Dennis Dart 8.5SDL/Carlyle B28F new as London Buses DT80 in September 1990. It was re-registered as 236 CLT in 1994, shortly before passing to the privatised London United company. It was re-registered as H880 LOX shortly before disposal to McKindless in 2000. It received fleet number D109, then became 880 before sale to First Stop Travel of Renfrew in 2003. It returned to McKindless in May 2006.

A729 YFS was a Leyland Olympian ONTL11/2R/ECW H51/32D new as Lothian Regional Transport number 729 in November 1983. On disposal it passed to HAD Coaches of Shotts for school contracts. On the collapse of HAD in 2004 it was picked up by McKindless and converted to single-door. It is seen at Bogside depot in one of the new pre-fabricated buildings used to upgrade the depot.

McKindless acquired a trio of Leyland Lynxes in the spring of 2000. E116 UTX was new to Merthyr Tydfil Transport, and is seen being prepared for service at Bogside depot. It was re-registered SIL 1813 prior to entering service. Production vehicles began to enter service in 1986. The majority were bodied by Leyland at its Workington factory, where the underframe was produced. Engines offered were the Leyland TL11, Gardner 6HLXCT and Cummins L10.

L152 WAG was a Dennis Dart/Plaxton Pointer B34F purchased new by London Buses as their DRL152 in August 1993. The company became South London Buses in January 1995, and Arriva London in April 2000. On disposal in March 2005 the bus passed to McKindless and was spotted operating in Eglinton Street in Glasgow while working on service 75.

K19 AMB was a Volvo B10M-60/Plaxton Premiere C46Ft purchased new by Amberline of Speke in 1992. It passed to Warrington Coachlines and was re-registered as 476 CEL, before joining the McKindless Group in 2006. It was seen descending North Hanover Street in Glasgow while working on the Glasgow Shuttle.

B298 WUL was an MCW Metrobus DR101/7 H71D purchased new by London Buses in August 1985 as their M1298. It joined McKindless from Arriva London in 2001 and was seen on the 75 service. These buses had their middle doors removed and an unglazed panel fitted to allow a two-seater bench to be fitted against the bulkhead.

J319 BVO was a DAF SB220/Optare Delta B49F new as Trent 319 in December 1991. It passed to the McKindless Group in 2001, and was passing through Hamilton while working on the 41 service to Lanark when seen. Around sixteen examples of this type would be amassed over the years. The Delta was launched in 1988 and production ceased in 1999, with a total of 324 being built.

The McKindless Group

P540 CTO was an Optare Excel L1150 B47F new to Nottingham City Transport as their fleet number 540 in October 1996. On disposal it passed to McKindless. The Excel was built in a range of lengths, and in Optare tradition the chassis code reflected this. An L960 was 9.6 metres in length; an L1000 was 10.0 metres in length, and so on; L1070 and L1150 variants were also built. Seating ranged from twenty-seven in the L960, to thirty-five in the L1070, forty-three in the L1150 and forty-five in the L1180, although these figures can vary. P540 CTO was pictured in Hamilton town centre.

KYV 702X was an MCW Metrobus DR101/14 H43/28D purchased new by London Transport as their fleet number M702 in November 1981. The MCW Metrobus was manufactured by Metro-Cammell Weymann (MCW) between 1977 and 1989, with over 4,000 units being built. They planned to produce a single-decker version, but this was not to be produced.

L166 YAT was a Dennis Dart 9SDL/Plaxton Pointer B34F new as London Buses DRL166 in 1994. Dennis Specialist Vehicles Limited, based in Guildford, was a major British manufacturer of specialised commercial vehicles. The company was best known as the manufacturer of fire engines, although other major product lines included buses, dustcarts and airport service vehicles. The brand continues to be used by several separate businesses: the bus construction business is part of Alexander Dennis; Dennis Eagle specialises in dustcart manufacture; and fire appliance body construction continues as John Dennis Coachworks, but using chassis and cabs from Volvo, MAN, Scania and others.

The company decided to have a small fleet of dedicated school buses and outshopped them in a yellow livery for safety. Additional hazard lights were also fitted between the decks and would flash when the buses were picking up or setting down pupils. KYV 772X, an MCW Metrobus, was snapped as it passed through Hamilton on its way back to Newmains depot after completing its run.

V898 DNB was a Dennis Dart SLF/Plaxton Pointer B29F purchased new by Davidson Buses of Bathgate in October 1999. It then passed to Stansted Transport before joining the McKindless fleet. It would later remain in Lanarkshire with Coakley/Mackenzie of Motherwell. When seen it was passing through Hamilton on service 41, bound for Lanark.

Towards the end of its existence the company acquired some more modern double-deckers for school contracts. G647 SGT began life as G111 NGN with London Buses as their fleet number VC11, and was a Volvo Citybus B10M-50/Northern Counties H47/35D. Meanwhile, E501 LFL was a Leyland Olympian ONLXCT/1RH/Optare CH43/27F that was new as Cambus number 501 in February 1988.

SN57 DXJ was an ADL Enviro 200 B29F purchased new by McKindless of Wishaw in December 2007. It is seen here in Motherwell town centre. On disposal it passed to Hunter's of Alloa. Note the wording on the destination screen, which was quite unusual. Nowadays the 41 service is run by JMB Travel, which uses similar, but longer buses on the route.

J711 CWT was a Volvo B10M-60/Plaxton Premiere C48Ft purchased new by Wallace Arnold Tours of Leeds in April 1992. On disposal it passed to Titterington's of Blencow, before joining McKindless in 2001. It was re-registered as YIB 1189 in June 2001, but for some unknown reason it then changed the same month to YIB 4528. This shot shows it being prepared for service at Bogside depot. It would receive full coach livery in due course.

R183 VLA was a Dennis Dart SLF/Plaxton Pointer B35F new as Metroline DL83 in June 1998. On disposal in February 2006 it was acquired by McKindless, and is shown freshly repainted as it passes through Hamilton. On the demise of the company it was snapped up by Coakley of Motherwell.

A busy scene in Glasgow city centre shows a pair of step-entrance Darts turning out of Union Street. By purchasing batches of similar buses, spare part holdings could be kept to a minimum and buses could be cannibalised to keep their sisters in service. The company's fleet was a common sight in the city for many years.

J945 MFT was a Dennis Dart 9.8SDL/Wright Handybus B40F new as Northern General number 8045 in June 1992. Many of these buses ended up in Scotland with various independents and provided some variety from the Plaxton-bodied examples in service. The grille has been picked out in black paint, which was not usually the case.

A124 XEP was a Leyland Tiger TRCTL11/3R/Duple Caribbean C50Ft purchased new by South Wales Transport as their 124 in April 1984. On disposal it passed to Irvine's of Law before reaching McKindless in 1996. It carried coach livery, which was based on the British Airways colours. It was leaving Glasgow's Buchanan bus station to work an evening peak journey on the express service to Newmains when captured.

L167 YAT was a Dennis Dart 9SDL/Plaxton Pointer B34F new as London Buses DRL167 in February 1994. It was bought by McKindless in September 2004, and was working in Clydebank on service 62 when seen. Vince used to joke that he did just what the bigger groups did by cascading buses from London, only they had no Scottish subsidiaries and he had no London presence.

G539 VBB was a Leyland Olympian ON2R/Northern Counties H47/27D purchased new by Kentish Bus as their fleet number 539 in March 1990. The company had won a batch of contracts for LRT that took them into the heart of Central London. A new operating base was found in Leyton, ready for services to start in January 1990. The routes involved were the 22A, 22B and 55, which were won from the London Forest district of London Buses. The bus was purchased by McKindless in 2006 and is shown in single-door format in Hamilton.

VRS 143L was a Daimler Fleetline CRL6-30/Alexander AL Type H45/29D new as Aberdeen Corporation number 143 in March 1973. It passed through the hands of Grampian Regional Transport before disposal. It worked for Northern Scottish and then Midland Scottish for around a week before it was transferred to Strathtay Scottish. It was then purchased by Highland Scottish. It was acquired by McKindless and collected from Stepps depot, but was captured at a yard they rented in Law Village for a spell.

POG 524Y was an MCW Metrobus DR102/27 H43/30F new as Midlands PTE number 2524 in October 1982. On disposal it passed to Thorpes of Perivale as their fleet number M534, before passing to McKindless in 2005. It was outshopped in school bus yellow and was caught at Parkhead depot in Glasgow.

P107 OLX was a Dennis Dart SLF/Plaxton Pointer B32F purchased new by Metroline as their DLS7 in June 1997. On disposal in December 2005 it passed to Stansted Transit. It joined McKindless of Wishaw the following year and went to Coakley in July 2010. It was photographed crossing Jamaica Bridge in Glasgow as it headed for the south side of the city.

KPJ 267W was a Leyland Atlantean AN68B/1R/Roe H43/30F new as London Country AN267 in April 1981. It joined the McKindless fleet in 1998, and was about to go out on a school contract for Holy Cross High School when seen. This style of bodywork was usually associated with Park Royal Coachbuilders of London, who were part of the same company.

G44 VME was a Leyland Lynx LX2R11 B49F new as Maidstone Boro'line number 811 in October 1989. It passed to Kentish Bus before disposal to Hall's of Kennoway. It joined the McKindless fleet in 2000 and was captured in Hamilton. The livery on this bus differed from the rest of the fleet, with more green on the front panels.

JTH 763P was a Leyland National 11351/1R B52F new to South Wales Transport as their number 763 in October 1975. It then passed to Northumbria, becoming number 736, where it was given a refurbishment. It joined McKindless and was being prepared for its duties the following day at Bogside depot. Note the strange destination boards that were briefly used.

C286 BBP was a Leyland Olympian ONLXB/1R/East Lancs CH43/27F new as Southampton Citybus 286 in April 1986. It passed to Midland Fox as their number 4482, then Sheffield Omnibus before reaching McKindless. It would later pass to Excel Logistics/Stansted Transit as a trade-in against some Dennis Darts.

K327 FAL was a DAF SB220L/Optare Delta B48F purchased new by Trent Barton as their fleet number 327 in August 1992. The DAF SB220 was a full-size single-decker chassis produced by DAF Bus International from 1985. Initially only built in left-hand drive, in 1988 a right-hand drive version was launched for the United Kingdom market. It would pass to McKindless in 2002, and was snapped in Motherwell town centre.

OJD 871R was a Leyland National 10351A/2R B36D new to London Transport as their LS71 in June 1977. On disposal in July 1993 it was bought by Stuart Palmer of Dunstable. It was resold in November 1993 to The Eden of West Auckland as their number N3, and was re-registered to RJI 5343 in February 1994. The Eden were taken over by United in 1996 and the bus became 3501 in that fleet. It later became Dart N21 as that company was part-owned by Arriva, and as such was able to access the group disposal sheets. It was bought by McKindless in February 1999.

L407 GDC was a Volvo B6-50/Plaxton Pointer B40F new to OK Travel in February 1994. It passed to Go Ahead with the business and received fleet number 8407, before sale to UK North of Gorton as their number 151. It was bought by McKindless in 2006, and was captured in Hamilton town centre.

C406 BUV was an MCW Metrobus DR101/17 H43/28D new as London Buses M1406 in November 1985. It passed to Arriva London before reaching McKindless in May 2005, and is seen at the company's Parkhead depot. Note the blank panel fitted over the centre doors, where a two-seat bench would be fitted. The bus would also be repainted into the yellow school bus livery.

L141 BFV was a Dennis Javelin 11SDL/Plaxton Premiere Interurban C47F new as Ribble number 141 in September 1993. It passed to Blazefield with part of Ribble's Lancashire operations. It was one of a pair taken into stock by McKindless in 2005, and was seen in Glasgow. On disposal it joined Forward Travel of Sampford Peverell, where it would be re-registered TJI 9141.

M188 UAN was a Dennis Lance SLF 11SDA/Berkhof B37D new to Speedlink Airport Services in July 1995. It passed to Menzies Aviation Services with the contract. The company was founded in 1833 when John Menzies opened a bookshop on Edinburgh's Princes Street. Following the turn of the millennium, Menzies acquired the global airport ground-handling operations of Ogden Aviation Services. This bus passed to McKindless in 2003 and was re-registered WIL 9207.

E408 RWR was a Volvo B10M-61/Duple 340 C55F new as Yorkshire Rider number 1408 in April 1988. On disposal it passed to Waddon's of Bedwas, then later became 772 URB. It moved to Newmark Coaches of Stratford as E386 AJC, before reaching McKindless in April 2000. It had a toilet installed, resulting in a reduced seating capacity of fifty-three, and was working on the Glasgow Shuttle when captured.

The McKindless Group

NEO 830R was a Leyland National 11351A/1R B49F new as Barrow Corporation number 12 in April 1977. In January 1989 an Administrative Receiver was appointed and on 26 May 1989 Barrow Borough Transport Ltd ceased to trade. The depot and twenty-four vehicles were taken over by Ribble, and these were later transferred to Cumberland. The bus was snapped up by McKindless in 1991, and was captured in Motherwell.

The Leyland Lynx (B60) was designed in 1984 as a replacement for the ageing Leyland National, being unveiled at the 1985 International Bus & Coach Exhibition at the Earls Court Exhibition Centre. The B60 was the first bus to carry the Lynx brand, but it was also used on lorries. A plan for offering this bus with a single-piece flat windscreen was considered, but was not carried out. A common feature, therefore, is that the Lynx has two separate windscreens with the driver's windscreen raked back, resembling 1950s single-decker buses and the Wright Handybus.

Bought new in 2006, BX56 XAP was a King Long 6113 B37F, which I always thought looked very attractive. It was photographed in Motherwell, heading for Lanark. It had quite a short life, however, and was later exported to Malta. Established in 1988, King Long United Automotive Industry Co. is one of the joint ventures in China with a long history in the coach manufacturing industry. The company is now jointly owned by Xiamen Automotive Industry Corporation, Xiamen State-owned Assets Investment Co. and San Yang Industry Co. from Taiwan, with the proportion of each shareholder being 50 per cent, 25 per cent and 25 per cent respectively.

RAU 809R was a Bristol VRT/ECW H74F purchased new by Midland General as their number 809 in December 1976. On disposal it passed to Northern Bus of Anston before joining Stuart's of Carluke. It moved up the road to McKindless and is seen near Newmains, heading out to do a school run for Morningside Primary.

The McKindless Group

NTN 870R was a Dennis F131 new to Tyne & Wear Fire Service in 1977. It was converted as a tow-wagon for the McKindless fleet, and was recovering a Dennis Dart from Glasgow city centre. Note the second crew door, which has been panelled over in true bus tradition, using a solid metal sheet.

SN57 DXH was an ADL Enviro 200 B29F purchased new by the company in December 2007, and was seen in Hamilton. On disposal it passed to Sullivan Buses as their AE2, and would be used around the Borehamwood area of London. The Enviro200 (originally referred to as the Enviro200 Dart) was supposed to be sized between a minibus and a large single-decker bus. It was originally designed as a replacement for the Dennis Dart SLF chassis and Alexander ALX200 and Plaxton Pointer 2 bodies.

H161 NON was a Dennis Dart 8.5SDL/Carlyle Dartline B28F new as London Buses DT161 in February 1991. In 1920 the Birmingham & Midland Motor Omnibus Company established a bus repair facility on land adjoining Rotton Park Reservoir. It initially performed repair work before chassis construction commenced in 1925. It derived its name from its address, Carlyle Road. In 1989, the body designs for the Duple Dartline were acquired from Trinity Holdings. In October 1991, Carlyle Works was placed in receivership and closed. The rights to the Dartline were sold to bodybuilder Marshall Bus.

NEO 831R was a Leyland National 11351A/1R B49F new as Barrow Borough Transport number 13 in April 1977. It was one of a batch taken into stock from Cumberland in 1991. The Stagecoach livery was simply adapted, with the stripes being overpainted in green. It was passing through Hamilton on service 66, bound for Shotts, when seen.

NDZ 3155 was a Dennis Dart 8.5SDL/Wright Handybus B29F new as London Buses DW155 in March 1993. It passed to Stagecoach East London the following year, then moved to Stagecoach Red & White as their number 455 in April 1998. It was re-registered as K996 CBO in 2003 and was sold to 2-Travel, Swansea, the following year. It was acquired by McKindless in December 2004, and was caught in Stockwell Street in Glasgow.

L53 CNY was a Volvo B10M-60/Plaxton Premiere C53F purchased new by Bebb of Llantwit Fardre in October 1993. It then passed to Alex Head Coaches of Lutton and was re-registered 52 GYY before reaching McKindless in 2005. Both it and Northern Counties-bodied Citybus G547 SGT next to it would pass to JMB Travel of Newmains, which would trade from the same premises and was incorporated on 18 February 2009.

K352 SCN was an Optare MetroRider MR03 B26F purchased new by Gateshead & District as their fleet number 352 in March 1993. A batch of four joined McKindless in 2001, and this one was loading in Motherwell town centre for Shotts on service 56 when captured. Note the extra cooling vents added to the engine cover.

GPT 94N was a Leyland National 11351/1R B49F delivered new as Northern General number 4518 in May 1974. On disposal it passed to Pride of the Road of Royston, before joining McKindless in 1991. It was an early recipient of the maroon and cream livery, as shown in this view taken at the company's Law premises.

H105 THE was a Dennis Dart 8.5SDL/Plaxton Pointer B28F new as London Buses DR5 in May 1991. It was purchased from London United by McKindless in 2000, and was seen passing through Motherwell. It is shown carrying an all-over advert for Untouchables, a DIY/wallpaper business established in Glasgow in 1990, which claims to be Scotland's largest wallpaper stockist.

MDV 692W was a Bedford YMT/Unicar C53F purchased new by Garrett of Newton Abbot in September 1980. It was a very early member of the McKindless fleet, and was snapped on a visit to the Glasgow Transport Museum, which was located in the Kelvin Hall at the time. Union Carrocera appointed Moseley Group (PSV) Ltd as its sole UK concessionaire for the model, which made its British debut at the Brighton Coach Rally in 1978.

EPT 883S was a Leyland National 11351A/1R B49F new as United 3083 in June 1978. It saw service with Beeston's of Hadleigh as PJI 4708 before its purchase by Vince McKindless in 1994. It was photographed here loading in Hamilton bus station. It would pass as their 1111 to Kelvin Central Buses with the services in 1994, but the McKindless Group would return, bigger and stronger.

R798 OYS started life on the Isle of Man as DNM 32R in 1997. It was a 10-metre Marshall Capital-bodied Dennis Dart SLF and was one of a batch of ten that joined the McKindless fleet in 2004. It was passing through Hamilton on the 31 service, bound for Lanark. Unlike the rest of the UK, Isle of Man Transport is owned by the Manx Government, and was founded on 1 October 1976 as an amalgamation of IOM Road Services and Douglas Corporation.

JST 107P was a Ford R1114/Alexander Y Type B53F purchased new by Highland Omnibuses in September 1975. It was acquired by McKindless during the Central SMT drivers' strike and was pressed into service in full Highland livery. This was later rectified and the mock Central livery was applied. These noisy, lightweight buses were far from ideal, with engine intrusion, high step heights and poor brakes.

P335 JND was a Volvo B6LE-53/Alexander ALX200 B36F new as Stagecoach Manchester 335 in February 1997. It later passed to Blazefield-owned Burnley & Pendle before joining the McKindless fleet in 2005. In 1991 Blazefield Travel was formed when Alan Stephenson's AJS Group sold seven bus companies, along with 300 buses and twelve depots, to two of its directors, Giles Fearnley and Stuart Wilde, in a management buyout.

Y393 LCS began life as 01-D-94170 with ComfortDelGro's Aircoach operations in Dublin. A dual-doored Plaxton Pointer-bodied Dennis Dart SLF dating from 2001, it passed to McKindless in 2007. It only seated thirty and had extra luggage racks, and was passing through Hamilton when snapped.

HDL 411N was a Bristol VRT/ECW H39/31F new as Southern Vectis 649 in May 1975. It joined the McKindless fleet in 1990, and was captured in Hamilton while working on service 66 to Newmains. The advert on the side panels was for Cooper Brothers, a family-owned business with three branches serving Lanarkshire. The company are still in business and recently celebrated their 50th anniversary.

Ex-London United Dennis Dart H105 THE receives attention at Bogside depot in Newmains. Its gloss paintwork has been buffed down to allow the new colours to adhere. The roof and rear of the bus have already been repainted. The depot had been steadily upgraded as finance allowed and hardstanding was being added in sections. The freehold had been purchased outright, using the cash from the sale of the service network to Kelvin Central Buses.

A67 GBN was a Leyland Tiger TRCTL11/3R/Plaxton Paramount 3500 C49F delivered new to the famous Yelloway of Rochdale fleet in June 1984. It passed to South Yorkshire PTE as their number 73 in 1986 and was given the cherished plate 3913 WE. It was re-registered yet again on disposal to Rigott of Kingsley in April 1996, this time to A361 BHL. McKindless acquired it the following year and it is shown in Glasgow.

Major investment was put into the Leyland National project when a batch of Volvo-engined buses were acquired from various sources and refurbished at Newmains. Work included updated back and front ends, new seating and destination slip-boards. Another feature was the grey advert panels, which would be sign-written for various local businesses, including some in-house advertising for McKindless baby shops, flower shops and wedding car hire.

G501 XBL was a DAF SB220L/Optare Delta B49F new as Reading Buses number 501 in September 1989. It was one of four purchased at the time, and was passing through Motherwell on service 9, bound for Hamilton, when seen. In September 1984, Leyland closed its Charles H. Roe bodywork-building business in Leeds. In response, Russell Richardson, a former plant director at Roe, backed by the West Yorkshire Enterprise Board and many redundant former employees, formed Optare in February 1985.

NEO 830R was a Leyland National 11351A/1R B49F new as Barrow Borough Transport number 12 in April 1977. The assets of the company were purchased by Stagecoach after a period of intense competition. It was originally placed under their Ribble subsidiary, but later became part of Cumberland after the territories were redrawn. The McKindless traffic manager had also come from Cumberland.

R93 HUS was an Optare Excel L1070 B39F delivered new to Hutchison's of Overtown in April 1998. It came to McKindless after the Hutchison business agreed to sell out to Firstbus. The agreement stated that this type should be offered for sale as Firstbus wasn't too keen to take them, but in the event of a failure to sell they would be part of the deal. Under normal circumstances it is exceedingly unlikely that Hutchison's would deal with McKindless as they were rivals.

A731 YFS was a Leyland Olympian ONTL11/2R/ECW H51/32D new as Lothian Regional Transport number 731 in November 1983. On disposal it passed to HAD Coaches of Shotts, the name coming from the initials of the founders, Harry and Deborah Law. The company collapsed and some buses were taken by the McKindless Group in 2001. This view was taken in Hamilton, and clearly shows the panelled-over middle door.

V190 DRC was an Optare Excel L1150 B43F new as Trent 190 in September 1999. It was purchased by McKindless in 2006. As part of the privatisation of the bus industry Trent was sold in a management buyout. In 1989 the business of Barton Transport was added and placed into a separate legal entity, even though both subsidiaries combined their operations on a day-to-day basis. The separate brands were brought together as 'Trent Barton' in 2005. A little-known fact is that Trent Barton maintains a 6 per cent shareholding in First Leicester.

Vincent McKindless kept a small heritage fleet, and Ford D series lorry KGD 871N stands beside AEC Routemaster ALD 966B at Newmains depot. The colours used were based on the former Central SMT bus company that served Lanarkshire up until 1989, and whose demise allowed the McKindless Group room to expand into stage carriage work.

AUP 359W was a Leyland Atlantean AN68B/1R/Roe H43/30F purchased new by Northern General as their fleet number 3459 in August 1980. On disposal in 1996 it joined OK Travel, but McKindless acquired it from Moordale of North Shields in February 1999 and allocated it fleet number DD450.

UEO 478T was a Leyland National 11351A/1R B49F new as Barrow-in-Furness Corporation number 16 in August 1978. Operations ceased on 26 May 1989, when, after a lengthy battle with Ribble Motor Services, the company ceased to trade. Stagecoach acquired some assets including this bus, which passed to McKindless in 1992. It was seen in Kirk Road in Wishaw while working on service 68, bound for Motherwell.

R694 OYS started life on the Isle of Man as DNM 35R in 1997 with IOM National Transport as their number 35. It was a Dennis Dart/Marshall Capital B37F, and was one of nine purchased by McKindless in 2004. The Marshall Capital was built between 1996 and 2002, and later by MCV between 2002 and 2003. Initially launched on the step-entrance MAN 11.220, and then the Iveco Eurorider chassis, the Capital found greater success after being launched on the low-floor Dennis Dart SLF chassis from 1997. Marshall also produced a related, integral midibus known as the Marshall Minibus between 1996 and 1998.

NAO 359M was a Leyland National 1151/1R B52F purchased new by Cumberland as their fleet number 359 in August 1973. It passed to McKindless and received this red and grey livery, as shown in this view taken in Hamilton. These buses featured the Leyland 510 fixed head engine. Sadly the 500 series was hastily developed and put into service with the design team's pleas for further proving falling on deaf ears. Senior BL management seemed quite happy with making the customers do the development work for them, a trend that continued throughout most of the '70s.

C637 SSB was a former MOD Bedford VAS5 fitted with a Wadham Stringer Vanguard body. It was sitting at Newmains depot in between school runs when photographed. In the early 1970s, the design of the VAS was considered obsolete; indeed, the far back door and the engine protruding into the interior complicated the implementation of one-man operation. However, many of the buses still found use with the armed forces, police and local authorities. It continued to be built in small numbers, until the closure of Bedford 1987.

DNW 843T was a Leyland National 10351B/1R B44F new as West Yorkshire 1005 in January 1979. It was transferred to Keighley & District as their number 255, then passed to Sovereign Bus and Coach as number 543, before acquisition by McKindless in 1997. It was loading in Kenilworth Avenue in Wishaw.

BX56 XAG was a BMC Falcon 1100 B40F delivered new to McKindless in November 2006, seen passing through Hamilton. Exports of Austin trucks from the UK to Turkey began in 1947. Austin merged with Morris Motors in 1952 to form the British Motor Corporation, or BMC for short. BMC Turkey was formed in 1964 in Izmir by Ergün Özakat in partnership with the British Motor Corporation. When exports to the United Kingdom began in 2003, this marked the return of BMC to the UK, with it not having been seen on British roads since the 1960s.

JDZ 2411 was a Dennis Dart 9SDL/Wright Handybus B35F new as London Buses DWL11 in December 1990. It was bought by McKindless in March 2000 and allocated fleet number D111. It was seen turning into Argyle Street in Glasgow city centre while working on service 56, bound for Shotts. It would later receive an electronic destination screen.

A rear view of one of the refurbished Leyland Nationals clearly shows that the back window has been panelled over, allowing a large fleet name to be displayed. The Volvo engines fitted were unfortunately heavier than the original Leyland units and caused some stress at the rear end.

The same bus as acquired, before any work was done on it. VKE 566S was a Leyland National 11351A/1R B49F new as Maidstone & District number 3566 in September 1977, later passing to Hastings & District. It later served with Lothian Buses after its life with McKindless, before entering preservation as a Hastings & District bus once again.

This former Blackpool Corporation Optare City Pacer was repainted into Express livery, and given the registration number JDZ 2403 for publicity photographs. I don't honestly know if it ever turned a wheel for the company as these buses had a very short life, due to reliability issues.

Former Highland Scottish Ford R1114 OST 255S was loading in Kenilworth Avenue in Wishaw while working on service 66, bound for Bonkle. The Fords were quickly replaced by more passenger-friendly Leyland Nationals, which were acquired from Stagecoach.

RFR 420P was a Leyland Atlantean AN68/1R/ECW H43/31F new as Ribble 1420 in June 1976. It passed to the neighbouring Cumberland fleet after their territories were redefined. It was later pressed into service in Lanarkshire in full Cumberland Stagecoach livery, and was loading in Hamilton on the 66 service, bound for Newmains, when spotted.

A selection of double-deckers await their next turn of duty at Newmains depot. The buses were usually well-presented and kept clean, which was not always an easy task in the winter, when salt is used to keep the roads clear of ice and snow. These were dedicated school buses fitted with fixed destinations.

FUG 325T was a Leyland National 10351B/1R B44F new as West Yorkshire number 1013 in March 1979. It passed to Sovereign Bus & Coach as their 325 before passing to McKindless in 1997 for the reintroduction of services. In 1978, Leyland brought out this model to replace the elderly Bristol LH, a type popular in NBC companies for rural routes. It was available in a single length (10.3 metres) and had a revised interior that had minimal lighting and was without the rear roof-mounted heating unit in previous models. Heating was under the seats, and was basic but effective.

ALD 966B was an AEC Routemaster/Park Royal H36/28R new as London Transport RM1966 in July 1964. It passed to Blackpool Transport as their number 529 in April 1988; it then became Reading Mainline number 44 in 1997 before joining McKindless for private hire work in November 1999. It was actually a gift for Vince's fiftieth birthday, hence the fleet number allocated to it – 1950. It was then purchased for preservation, but returned to service with The London Bus Company in June 2013.

JMJ 148V was a Ford R1114/Duple Dominant II purchased new by Whites of Camberley in January 1980. It passed to McKindless during 1992 from Pratt of Carluke, and was actually working on hire to Haldanes of Cathcart when seen.

A563 KWY was a Leyland Olympian ONLXB/1R/ECW CH42/28F new as West Riding number 563 in September 1983. It passed to Tees & District as their number 0243 before the company was subsumed into Arriva North East. It joined the McKindless fleet in 1999, and was working on the Glasgow Shuttle when photographed.

F124 PHM was a Volvo Citybus B10M-50/Alexander RV Type H46/29D purchased new by Cowie, t/a Grey Green, as their 124 in October 1988. The company became Arriva London before the bus passed to MK Metrobus. It joined the McKindless fleet and was used as a dedicated school bus. On the demise of the company it passed to JMB Travel of Newmains, then Dunn's of Airdrie.

The McKindless Group

D140 NUS was a Mercedes L608D/Alexander B21F new as Kelvin Scottish 1140 in October 1986. On disposal it went to Kirkby Lonsdale Coach Hire. It returned to Scotland to join the fledgling Dart Buses of Paisley fleet, before its sale to McKindless of Wishaw in 1997. It is shown with decals for service 68, but it had a short life and was withdrawn in 1998.

The Routemaster had its livery altered to allow it to advertise Scotch whisky. It had the shade of red digitally altered to look like a London bus, and was driven to the Highlands for filming. This was pieced together with film of a similar bus in London to make it look like the same bus. Note the legal lettering, which was for McKindless Express.

RFM 884M was a Leyland National 1151/1R B49F new as Crosville SNL884 in January 1974. It passed to East Midland before transferring to Perth Panther. It was acquired by McKindless and pressed into service in Stagecoach livery, as shown in this view taken in Wishaw.

The depot at Parkhead was located in Nuneaton Street and was a very modern building, having only been completed in 2005, and was built to replace Rutherglen depot. The premises later passed to a plant hire company. Here, Optare Delta G507 XBL keeps Leyland Olympian G536 VBB company.

R817 OYS was a Dennis Dart 10.7M Marshall Capital B37F, which began life as Isle of Man National Transport number 29, with Manx registration number R29 DMN. It passed to McKindless in 2004 and was caught in Glasgow on service 80 from Harestanes. On the demise of the company the bus would pass to Vale Travel, which was part of GHA Coaches. They ceased trading after entering administration on 13 July 2016.

An ex-London step-entrance Dennis Dart goes head-to-head with First Glasgow Scania S701 BFS as they cross Jamaica Bridge in Glasgow. They will both follow the same route to Kennishead via Shawlands Cross. The McKindless bus certainly wasn't troubled by passengers, and the route was a systematic failure. The drivers didn't seem to go out of their way to get passengers and would often let Firstbus clear the busy stops before streaming ahead.

MCW Metrobus B299 WUL was a very late repaint, and used a version of the livery normally reserved for single-deckers. The use of the new style of fleet name was also unusual on a double-decker. The company seemed to be on its knees by this time, and one must wonder why a new style of fleet name was introduced!

C601 LFT was a Leyland Olympian ONLXB/1R/Alexander RH Type H45/32F new as Tyne & Wear PTE Number 601 in November 1985. It passed to Stagecoach with the business and was later transferred to Glasgow. On disposal in 2007 it joined the McKindless fleet, along with six sister buses, and was captured as such in Motherwell town centre.